I0458933

Published by Daoudi Publishing LLC
ISBN: 978-1-960809-30-8

Cat
I Keep
Searching for
Answers...

A Remembrance and Grief Journal
with Therapeutic Writing Prompts for
Emotional Healing After the Loss of a Cat
(An Open Letter for Bereaved Pet Lovers)

Evelyn Harrington

I Keep Searching for Answers Journals

TABLE OF CONTENTS

INTRODUCTION

By Evelyn Harrington

Grief is not just about loss, it's about learning to live with love that has nowhere to go. if you are holding this journal, know that whatever you're feeling is valid. the pain, the questions, the memories, and even the silence, all of it deserves space.

Losing a cat changes everything. you may find yourself searching for answers, replaying moments, or wishing for words left unspoken. you may feel overwhelmed or unsure of what to feel at all. that's okay. grief isn't a straight path, and healing isn't about forgetting, it's about making room for what you carry inside.

This journal is here to support you, offering a safe space to express, reflect, and process at your own pace. the prompts inside will help you navigate loss, honor your emotions, and remind you that you are not alone.

Write when you're ready. be honest with yourself. your story, your grief, and your love for your dog will always matter.

With warmth and understanding,
Evelyn Harrington

HOW TO USE THIS JOURNAL

There is no right or wrong way to use this journal. Some prompts may feel natural to answer, while others may be difficult. That's okay. If a prompt feels too heavy, you can:

- Write without stopping for one minute. don't worry about grammar, structure, or making sense. just let your thoughts pour onto the page, unfiltered.

- Pause and take a deep breath. give yourself permission to feel without judgment.

- Write from someone else's perspective. imagine what your loved one might say to you, or how a friend would respond to your emotions.

- Read the prompt out loud. saying the words first can help you process them before writing anything down.

IF YOU EVER FEEL STUCK, START WITH:

- Write down what you can answer today. if a prompt feels too big, break it down. answer just a small piece, and leave the rest for another time. some prompts may feel easier with time.

This journal is here for you, without expectations or timelines. Use it at your own pace, in whatever way helps you process your loss. Every word, every pause, and every tear matters.

This Journal Belongs To:

_____

Still With Me

The house is quiet, the days move slow,

But in small ways, you let me know.

A purr, a paw, the naps we made,

Still echo where your love has stayed.

The scent of rain, a gentle breeze,

The way you leapt beneath the trees.

A whispered thought, a lullaby song,

Reminds me that your love is strong.

Though grief remains, I sometimes find

Your spirit lives within my mind.

And in those moments, calm and near,

I feel you, Cat, forever here.

DEALING WITH THE SHOCK OF LOSS

"Grief is the price we pay for love."
— Queen Elizabeth II

Dear cat, ever since the shock of losing you, i've had a hard _____

_____

_____

_____

I felt like everything around me _____

_____

_____

_____

There was a moment when i felt completely numb, like _____

_____

_____

I didn't know what to do, so i just _____

_____

_____

I keep waiting for someone to tell me that _____

_____

_____

_____

DEALING WITH THE SHOCK OF LOSS

"It hurts because it mattered."
— John Green

It hit me the hardest when i saw _____
_____
_____

The first time it truly hit me that you were gone was when _____
_____
_____

I couldn't stop shaking when _____
_____
_____
_____

My body still remembers _____
_____
_____
_____

I didn't know what to do, so i just _____
_____
_____
_____

ACCEPTING THE TRUTH LITTLE BY LITTLE

"Denial is a cushion we land on before we're ready to stand."
— Unknown

Dear cat, i keep telling myself this didn't really happen and _____

_____

_____

Some days, i still think you're just_____

_____

_____

_____

I don't want to believe that i'll never _____

_____

_____

It feels like you're just away for a while, like _____

_____

_____

_____

I tell myself that maybe you're just _____

_____

_____

_____

ACCEPTING THE TRUTH LITTLE BY LITTLE

"Denial is the shock absorber for the soul. It protects
us until we are capable of handling the truth."
— Unknown

It still feels like you'll walk through the door and _____

_____

_____

_____

I've avoided looking at _____

_____

_____

I still talk to you sometimes like you're right here and i say ____

_____

_____

It doesn't feel real that you're not here when i _____

_____

_____

_____

I pretend everything is normal when _____

_____

_____

_____

A Special Moment Together

Place for Photo

Place for Photo

Place for Photo

A Space for Cherished Memories

SORTING THROUGH CONFUSING THOUGHTS

"It's okay to be confused. Confusion is the route to all clarity."
— Shannon L. Alder

My cat, i feel like i should know how to handle _____

_____

_____

I don't understand why _____

_____

_____

_____

I'm confused about why_____

_____

_____

_____

I wish someone could explain _____

_____

_____

I feel like i'm _____

_____

_____

_____

SORTING THROUGH CONFUSING THOUGHTS

*"When you're lost in those woods, it sometimes
takes you a while to realize that you are lost."*
— Patrick Ness

I thought i understood life, but now_____

_____

_____

_____

I keep looking for answers about_____

_____

_____

_____

Some days, i feel okay, but then_____

_____

_____

I don't know why i feel_____

_____

_____

It feels like my emotions change every day because_____

_____

_____

_____

FACING FEAR AND MOVING FORWARD

"Fear has two meanings: Forget Everything And Run
or Face Everything And Rise. The choice is yours."
— Zig Ziglar

Dear cat, since you've been gone, i'm afraid that _____

_____

_____

Some days, i wake up afraid that _____

_____

_____

_____

I'm afraid of facing _____

_____

_____

_____

I worry that i'll never be able to _____

_____

_____

I keep thinking about the future and wondering _____

_____

_____

_____

FACING FEAR AND MOVING FORWARD

*"I learned that courage was not
the absence of fear, but the triumph over it."*
— Nelson Mandela

I don't know what scares me more, missing you or _____

_____

_____

I wish i could_____

_____

_____

_____

I'm scared that life without you will always feel _____

_____

_____

_____

Dear cat , if you were here, i know_____

_____

_____

_____

_____

_____

HANDLING ANGER IN A HEALTHY WAY

"Holding onto anger is like drinking poison
and expecting the other person to die."
— Buddha

My cat, i get mad at myself when _____

_____

_____

_____

I get angry sometimes when i see other people with their cats

_____

_____

_____

_____

_____

I never thought i'd be this mad about _____

_____

_____

_____

It makes me mad that i didn't realize how precious _____

_____

_____

_____

HANDLING ANGER IN A HEALTHY WAY

"Letting go of anger doesn't mean forgetting, it means choosing peace over pain."
— Unknown

I hate that i don't have _____

_____

_____

_____

I just want you to know that _____

_____

_____

_____

When people tell me _____

_____

_____ i feel like _____

_____

_____

I know i should focus on healing _____

_____

_____

_____

_____

LETTING GO OF REGRET AND "WHAT-IFS"

"Let go of what you think you should've done. You did
what you could with what you had."
— Unknown

Dear cat, i feel guilty that i didn't _____

_____

_____

I feel like i failed you when _____

_____

_____

_____

If i had just one more day with you, i would _____

_____

_____

I regret the times i was too busy to _____

_____

_____

_____

I feel guilty that i didn't _____

_____

_____

_____

LETTING GO OF REGRET AND "WHAT-IFS"

"Guilt is always hungry, don't let it consume you."
— Terri Guillemets

I wish i had listened more when someone told me to:

• I worked on making _____

_____

• I reminded myself that _____

_____

• I held on to _____

_____

• I learned to _____

_____

• It was time to stop _____

_____

• I needed to live _____

_____

• I needed to trust that _____

_____

• I tried to figure out how to _____

_____

FREE YOURSELF FROM SHAME

"The less you talk about your shame, the more power it has."
— Brené Brown

Dear cat, sometimes i feel ashamed because _____

_____

_____

I feel embarrassed when people see me_____

_____

_____

I know i shouldn't _____

_____

_____

_____

If you were here, i know you'd _____

_____

_____

_____

I struggle to talk about_____

_____

_____

_____

FREE YOURSELF FROM SHAME

"Shame dies when stories are told in safe places."
— Unknown

I avoid certain people because i'm afraid they'll think _____

_____

_____

_____

Sometimes i catch myself lying about _____

_____

_____

_____

I feel uncomfortable talking about you because i'm afraid people

will think _____

_____

_____

Even though i know you'd understand, i want to let myself feel

these natural feelings of shame and _____

_____

_____

_____

BREAKING THE SILENCE

"Speak your truth, even if your voice shakes."
— Maggie Kuhn

My cat, even when we disagreed, i always hoped you knew

_____

_____

_____

I wish we could go back to that day when _____

_____

_____

I'll never know why you couldn't _____

_____

_____

_____

I wanted you to see the real me when _____

_____

_____

_____

There were things i never said because i was afraid you'd _____

_____

_____

BREAKING THE SILENCE

"There is no greater agony than bearing an untold story inside you."
— Maya Angelou

I still question why you _____

_____

_____

_____

I held back my feelings for so long because i thought you'd _____

_____

_____

_____

I hope you knew that even in the worst moments, i still _____

_____

_____

_____

I forgive you for all _____

_____

_____

_____

Forever in This Frame

Place for Photo

Place for Photo

Place for Photo

A Collection of Wise Lessons

_____

_____

_____

_____

_____

_____

_____

_____

_____

_____

_____

_____

_____

_____

_____

_____

_____

_____

_____

_____

COPING WITH FEELING ALONE

"Healing begins when you realize you're not the only one who feels this way."
— Unknown

My cat, since you've been gone, i feel so alone _____

_____

_____

I miss having you here when _____

_____

_____

_____

Sometimes i sit in the quiet and pretend you're still _____

_____

_____

_____

I don't know how to fill the space you left when _____

_____

_____

Some nights, i lie awake thinking about _____

_____

_____

_____

COPING WITH FEELING ALONE

"The eternal quest of the human being is to shatter loneliness."
— Norman Cousins

Dear cat, i feel invisible because no one seems to notice that

_____

_____

No one really understands how much i _____

_____

_____

There are times when i want to talk to you so badly, but instead, i

just _____

_____

I miss the way you listened when i spoke about:

♦ _____

♦ _____

♦ _____

♦ _____

♦ _____

It feels like the world has moved on, but i _____

_____

_____

MANAGING DEEP SADNESS

"It's okay to cry. It's okay to not be okay. Just don't give up."
— Unknown

Dear cat, there are days when sadness follows me everywhere,

especially on the days when _____

_____

_____

Even when i'm surrounded by people, i feel the sadness_____

_____

_____

I find myself crying when i think about _____

_____

_____

Some nights, i hold my breath, wishing you'd _____

_____

_____

_____

There are moments when i try _____

_____

_____

_____

MANAGING DEEP SADNESS

"Let your sadness speak. Your heart has something it wants you to hear."
— Unknown

It hurts to think about the things you'll never get to see, like:

- ◆ _____
- ◆ _____
- ◆ _____
- ◆ _____
- ◆ _____
- ◆ _____
- ◆ _____
- ◆ _____
- ◆ _____
- ◆ _____

I know you wouldn't want me to be this sad, but _____

_____

_____

If you were here, i know you'd _____

_____

_____

_____

HOLDING THE MEMORIES

"There are places in the heart that can only be filled with memories."
— Unknown

My cat, i miss the way you always knew exactly what i wanted

when _____

_____

I still remember the day i brought you home _____

_____ and _____

You always knew how to make me smile, whether it _____

_____

_____ or _____

Sweet cat, i miss the way we used to drive around listening to

_____ and _____

and _____

I still remember the days we played _____

_____

_____ until it got dark.

I still remember the times i let you stay _____

_____

_____ and eating _____

and drinking _____ like it was a party.

HOLDING THE MEMORIES

"Sometimes, only one person is missing, and the whole world seems depopulated."
— Alphonse de Lamartine

You always made sure i felt special, even _____

_____

_____

I still remember how we sat together in the living room, your

eyes fixed on me with pure love, or when_____

_____ or _____

_____ like there was no rush.

I still think about how i took the time to teach you how to

_____

_____ making you feel capable and strong.

I still remember how i took you shopping and let you_____

_____ and _____

_____ and _____

_____

Dear cat, i loved how we used to go on trips to _____

_____ and _____

_____ and _____

_____ always making the best memories outdoors.

32

Memories That Last

Place for Photo

Place for Photo

Place for Photo

Place for Photo

Moments and Things That Keep
Cat's Memory Alive

_____

_____

_____

_____

_____

_____

_____

_____

_____

_____

_____

_____

_____

_____

_____

_____

_____

_____

_____

_____

_____

_____

FINDING SMALL MOMENTS OF PEACE

"The moment of relief is when you realize you don't have to carry it all alone."
— Unknown

Dear cat, i know you're no longer in pain, and that brings me

some peace because _____

_____

_____

There's comfort in knowing your _____

_____

_____

Letting go of the pain doesn't mean _____

_____

_____

_____

Knowing you're at peace makes it a little easier to _____

_____

_____

Even when i cry, i also feel relief _____

_____

_____

_____

FINDING SMALL MOMENTS OF PEACE

"Breathe. Let go. And remind yourself that this very moment is the only
one you know you have for sure."
— Oprah Winfrey

Dear cat, i can finally sleep a little better knowing that _____

_____

_____

Sometimes, i close my eyes and feel you near, and that brings me

_____

_____

Even in my hardest moments _____

_____

_____

I take a deep breath and feel a strange sense of relief when
i remember that you're _____

_____

_____

I used to be so afraid of losing you, but now i realize _____

_____

_____

MAKING ROOM FOR ACCEPTANCE

"Happiness can exist only in acceptance."
— George Orwell

Beloved cat, i will always love you, but i am learning to live with

_____

_____

It's taken me time, but i finally understand that _____

_____

_____

_____

I have learned to be grateful for_____

_____

_____

_____

Even though i'll always miss you, i am _____

_____

_____

I used to think i couldn't go on without you, but now i know

_____

_____

_____

MAKING ROOM FOR ACCEPTANCE

"Understanding is the first step to acceptance, and only with
acceptance can there be recovery."
— J.K. Rowling

Sweet cat, i am beginning to see that you will always be with me
when _____

_____

_____

I'm slowly learning to let go of what i can't change and _____

_____

_____

I'm starting to understand that love and loss can exist _____

_____

_____

_____

I'm accepting that healing happens in small steps, like _____

_____

_____

_____

I trust that my heart can hold both grief and _____

_____

_____

HONORING THE PAST WITH GRATITUDE

"Gratitude is not only the greatest of virtues, but the parent of all others."
— Marcus Tullius Cicero

Even though you're gone, i am thankful that i can still _____

_____

_____

I am grateful for the strength you gave me, especially when i

_____

_____

Your kindness and wisdom still guide me when _____

_____

_____

I will always be thankful for the lessons you taught me, like:

◆ _____

◆ _____

◆ _____

◆ _____

◆ _____

◆ _____

◆ _____

◆ _____

HONORING THE PAST WITH GRATITUDE

"The more grateful I am, the more beauty I see."
— Mary Davis

My cat, i feel gratitude when i think about how much you

_____

_____

I appreciate the way you shaped my life by _____

_____

_____

Every time i think of you, i remember to be thankful for _____

_____

_____

I want to thank you for:

- ◆ _____
- ◆ _____
- ◆ _____
- ◆ _____
- ◆ _____
- ◆ _____
- ◆ _____

KEEPING CAT'S LOVE IN YOUR HEART

"The love we give away is the only love we keep."
— Elbert Hubbard

Dear cat, i will always love you _____

_____

_____

One of the greatest gifts of your love was _____

_____

_____

I still feel your love when _____

_____

_____

_____

I see the love you gave me reflected in _____

_____

_____

_____

I carry your love with me every day, especially when _____

_____

_____

_____

KEEPING CAT'S LOVE IN YOUR HEART

"Where there is love there is life."
— Mahatma Gandhi

I hope i make you proud _____

_____

_____

Your love taught me how to _____

_____

_____

Your love still guides me when i have to _____

_____

_____

_____

I think of you every time i hear_____

_____

_____

_____ because it reminds me of your love.

If i could hug you one more time, i'd say_____

_____

_____

_____

A Photo of Love and Laughter

Place for Photo

Place for Photo

Place for Photo

Place for Photo

Place for Photo

Place for Photo

A Frame for Meaningful Advice

FINDING HOPE EVEN ON HARD DAYS

"Hope is being able to see that there is light despite all of the darkness."
— Desmond Tutu

Dear cat, i find hope in knowing that one day, i will _____

_____

_____

_____

I am starting to see signs, like:

- ◆ _____
- ◆ _____
- ◆ _____
- ◆ _____
- ◆ _____

There was a time when i thought i'd never feel okay again, but now

_____

_____

_____

Even on my hardest days, i remind myself that _____

_____

_____

_____

FINDING HOPE EVEN ON HARD DAYS

"Once you choose hope, anything's possible."
— Christopher Reeve

I know you'd tell me to keep dreaming, so i will _____

_____

_____

_____

I'm starting to believe that joy can exist alongside _____

_____

_____

I will carry your lessons with me as i step into _____

_____

_____

I hope i can make you proud by _____

_____

_____

_____

I am looking forward to _____

_____

_____

_____

HEALING AND STRENGTH

"Growth is painful. Change is painful. But nothing is as painful as staying stuck somewhere you don't belong."
— Mandy Hale

Sweet cat, through this journey, i have learned to appreciate

_____

_____

_____

I have learned about my own strength because _____

_____

_____

_____

I never imagined i could heal in this way, but i am starting to

_____

_____

I have become more patient with myself and _____

_____

_____

Dear cat, i never thought i'd be able to _____

_____

_____

_____

HEALING AND STRENGTH

"Be not afraid of growing slowly, be afraid only of standing still."
— Chinese Proverb

I have realized that growth comes from: _____

_____

_____

My support system includes: _____

- ◆ _____
- ◆ _____
- ◆ _____
- ◆ _____
- ◆ _____
- ◆ _____
- ◆ _____
- ◆ _____

If you were here, i know you'd remind me that strength is _____

_____

_____

_____

SELF-CARE WHILE YOU HEAL

"Act as if what you do makes a difference. It does."
— William James

To improve my daily life, i plan to focus on my sleep, meals, and

exercise, so i can _____

_____

_____

I plan to set a consistent sleep schedule by going to bed at _____

_____ and waking up at _____

To improve my sleep, i'll avoid _____

_____

_____ before bed and instead focus on _____

_____

_____

My plan for improving my appetite is to start each day with

a healthy breakfast like _____

_____

_____

To boost my appetite, i'll try eating smaller portions of_____

_____

_____throughout the day.

SELF-CARE WHILE YOU HEAL

"The journey of a thousand miles begins with one step."
— Lao Tzu

My goal for a balanced appetite is to include _____

_____

_____

_____ in my meals.

I plan to schedule time for sports activities like _____

_____

_____ at least _____ times a week.

To make exercise enjoyable, i'll combine sports with fun activities

like _____

_____

To improve my physical and mental health, i'll incorporate sports

such as _____

_____

_____ into my weekly routine.

I plan to use sports as a way to manage stress by _____

_____

_____

_____ whenever i feel overwhelmed.

YOU ARE NOT ALONE ON THIS JOURNEY

(A GENTLE MESSAGE FOR BEREAVED PEOPLE)

"One kind word can warm three winter months."
— Japanese Proverb

You are not alone in this. we will find our way through this grief, together and _____

_____

You don't have to be strong every moment. some days, just breathing is enough and _____

_____

_____

When the world feels like it has moved on, i want you to know

_____

_____

It's okay if you still expect to hear your cat's voice or see them walk through the door, this _____

_____

You don't have to feel okay all the time, but when peace finds you, even for a moment, let yourself _____

_____

_____

YOU ARE NOT ALONE ON THIS JOURNEY

(A GENTLE MESSAGE FOR BEREAVED PEOPLE)

"The best way to find yourself is to lose yourself in the service of others."
— Mahatma Gandhi

Some days, acceptance will feel impossible, and other days, it will feel like a quiet understanding. both are part of healing, just _____

_____

_____

You might feel lost right now, but i promise you, one day, you will find _____

_____

Every memory, every lesson, every moment you shared is a gift that will always be yours. let gratitude be your _____

_____

_____

Even in solitude, you are connected to those who love you _____

_____

_____

Drink water, get fresh air, and find small ways to take care _____

_____

_____

A Memory Captured for Me

Place for Photo

Place for Photo

Place for Photo

This Is My Healing Story

_____

_____

_____

_____

_____

_____

_____

_____

_____

_____

_____

_____

_____

_____

_____

_____

_____

_____

Echoes of You

I hear your paws in morning rain,

In quiet rooms that speak your name.

You're in the hush before the dawn,

A gentle love that still lives on.

I miss your purr, your tender face,

The little joys I can't replace.

But in the stillness soft and wide,

Your memory stays by my side.

Though life has changed and time moved through,

My heart still beats with love for you.

And in the wind or fading skies,

Your precious spirit never dies.

THE END

By Evelyn Harrington

Thank you for allowing this journal to be a part of your journey.
If you've filled these pages, even a little, know that you have already
taken steps toward healing. if you found yourself pausing, struggling,
or needing to step away, that's okay too. healing is not about
speed, it's about giving yourself grace in the moments you need it most.

I wrote this journal with the hope that it would offer you comfort,
reflection, and a safe space to express what's inside. no words will ever
replace the presence of the one you lost, but i hope you have found
a way to hold their love close, through your thoughts, your memories,
and your own path forward.

I Am Grateful to You

If this journal has helped you in any way, i would be truly grateful
for your support. Leaving a review, sharing your experience, or
recommending this journal to someone in need allows more people
to find comfort and healing through these pages. your words have the
power to help others, just as your journey has value in ways you may
not yet realize.

With warmth and understanding,
Evelyn Harrington